THE CATCH

POETRY

Folding the Real
Travel Diary
The Distance Between Us
Common Prayer
Rough Music
Night Fugue: New and Selected Poems
Coleshill

NON-FICTION

The Self on the Page (with Celia Hunt)
The Healing Word
A Fine Line: New poetry from Central and Eastern Europe
  (with Jean Boase-Beier & Alexandra Buchler)
Creative Writing in Health and Social Care
Writing: Self and Reflexivity (with Celia Hunt)
On Listening
Poetry Writing
A Century of Poetry Review (editor)
Music Lessons: Newcastle Bloodaxe Poetry Lectures
Percy Bysshe Shelley (editor)
Beyond the Lyric: A Map of Contemporary British poetry

AS TRANSLATOR

Evening Brings Everything Back by Jaan Kaplinski
Day by Amir Or

THE CATCH

Fiona Sampson

Chatto & Windus
LONDON

1 3 5 7 9 10 8 6 4 2

Chatto & Windus, an imprint of Vintage,
20 Vauxhall Bridge Road,
London SW1V 2SA

Chatto & Windus is part of the Penguin Random House group of companies
whose addresses can be found at global.penguinrandomhouse.com

Penguin
Random House
UK

Copyright © Fiona Sampson 2016

First published by Chatto & Windus in 2016

www.vintage-books.co.uk

A CIP catalogue record for this book is available from the British Library

ISBN 9781784740658

Typeset by Palimpsest Book Production Ltd, Falkirk, Stirlingshire

Printed and bound in Great Britain by Clays Ltd, St Ives plc

Penguin Random House is committed to a sustainable future for our business,
our readers and our planet. This book is made from Forest Stewardship
Council® certified paper

MIX
Paper from
responsible sources
FSC
www.fsc.org   FSC® C018179

for Peter

Like a singing catch, some are beginning when others are ending.

— SIR WILLIAM CORNWALLIS

Contents

A PATH BETWEEN THE TREES

THE CATCH

Wake

Wake again to first light
it's like a slim cat
coming home through Top Field
through high barley scarcely shifting
tassels scarcely
parting stems that stay half hidden
in a dark
that won't give up the night
where roots go down
any which way here's another
feet fall feet lift
nothing to it.

The Border

One after another they
reveal themselves
stepping solemnly
into the light

creatures great and small
all of them strangers
all of them naked as the white
moths that skitter

round them
only half surfacing
from the deep dream place
where they live

and from where they greet you
emissaries
who arrive out of dark hedges
gradually

like sight clearing
or all at once
who stand and wait to address
your bright path

knowing themselves seen
in the headlights
but not by whom staring through you
as if star-struck

and you too inside the car
your hands dark
on the wheel your dark
eyes wide

haven't you arrived
once again at
astonishment
at the brink of dream?

At Bleddfa

Back and forth
all morning
through the door the dogs
wander like clouds

nudging each other
pondering
a long dream
familiars

of the kitchen
as of the wet and sunny grass
they settle things
into place

chairs in order
boots by the door
all *sachlichkeit*
and they remind me

how when I was
still a child
my father took me
to a friend's house

empty attics
wooden stairs
and a garden slung
between elms

where rooks called
I was afraid
and not afraid
of how the day hung

above the still house
how in my mind
there was nothing
but a stilled sky.

Neighbours

Sound arrives in waves
but the voices
of my neighbours
at the paddock gate

arrive clear and baffled
by grass
as they've sounded all my life
singular

and clear
voices in the great room
of outdoors voices
that will guide me

when I'm old as when
in early memory
they arrived
while I was lost

among the gold and green
in a garden
with snapdragons
and with pansies –

lion faces
black and gold
these were new
as I was new.

Daily Bread

Sometimes it's just the daily bread
of thought just the visible
being itself (a cup of coffee
carried to a window seat

where varnished woodwork shines
in the morning light) sometimes
small things reveal to you
how you're alive and how you live

sometimes there's no remission
no trumpet no voice of God
in Levantine splendour only
this blur of steam like a breath

and the word lying below it
waiting to be spoken you can't
quite make it out what is it
humming all day out of hearing.

Stroke

Maybe five minutes
you lay on your back
wedged like greedy Alice
across the too-small landing
as I counted your breaths

Maybe five minutes
my hand tilting your head back
you breathing and smiling
eyes liquid and bright as if
something was dissolving them

Late

Not much use
saying then
I was busy
I was asked

as if to suggest
there were orders
I only followed
useless afterwards

when you find
it was your life
you murdered
your own life

that mobile
muscled thing so sweet
to hold
but always slipping

out of your arms
grasping
and letting slip
you thought

it would outlast you
with its promise
and clean flesh
sometimes

you grasped air
but you thought
that there would always be
this other thing

beyond the body
beyond soul even
keeping you
company somewhere

not quite forgotten
not quite held
in mind persisting
all the same.

Stucco

That's how it is
                    a bright patch of wall
then the window shuts

But in that moment
the light on the yellow wall is a voice
speaking to you quite distinctly

Drowned Man

See how they sleep first he turns
away and then she turns
after him or now she turns
her back and he follows

rolled by an imperative
deeper than sleep
he rolls over like a wave
that turns itself over

sleepily with the sea's deep
breathing with its rhythm
pulsing far out from land pulsing far
down in the dark

where creatures not yet formed are forming
where like half made beasts
his dreams swim among hers where
she hears his breathing far

above her nearer to the light
nearer to the white-topped
waves the white-peaked sheets his arm
thrown across her now

as she floats upward drawing him
out of deep tides crossing
their legs once more and morning lies
motionless to the horizon.

Rite

They make their way
across the fields
where snow lies
like rubble
they're singing
at least you think
that's what you hear
the wind carries
voices up
and down they carry
objects you're
too far away
to make out they
do not go smoothly
over the snow
over the rubble
of winter
sometimes they pause
and seem to gesture
or they could
be dancing
from here it's too far
to see too cold
too long ago
our forefathers
and mothers
making their way
as if towards
us as if
towards some other
destination.

Dante's Cave

Velika Dolina, Škocjan

Finally I came
to the end of the world
to a limestone cliff
falling in pale steps

and far below a pool
somehow out of myth
proving that there
was nothing but the rock

to hold me up to raise me
into that clear air
where crows were looping where the eye
of God was gold

and inattentive then
I saw the end is air
and falling it is clean
and lovely it is blue.

Visitors

When the horses came to visit
strange guests
eating the compost spreading
its scraps and colours

too big and sudden
curious neighbours
stepping awkwardly
along the path sniffing the roses

when they visited us
early in the morning
snapping the fence rail coming
in across the ditch

mild yet certain
in the way of dreams
and we answered their
summons stepping out

barefoot among the roses
with our own dreams
and the smells of sleep
still clinging to us

half awake
we saw ourselves as they had dreamt us
walking between them
as they walked between us.

Clothesline

Warmth and wet
rise in clouds from the clean sheets
everything lifted

as if on hoists
into a new
smell of water

I will swim down to the river
arm over arm among slips
and sheets and pearled river lights

Street Music

Wind in the streets wind
that you remember
under the bedroom window
wonderingly

it recited something
that you knew
now it tells
how you know nothing it says

you are still a child
the smallest person
in the room the one
who hears the wind

along the pavement
wind shaking the hedge
and the cherry branches
shaking the glass

so the lamplight from the street
breaks
so all the shining things
tremble and break.

The Hunters

These black and matted crowns these gold
shadows you who think
you see but who do not come
seeking the death at
the valley's lip the blast the leap

(says the hunter) you
who do not worship with a sacrifice
as we have always
sacrificed what can you know
of the trees' secrets

or of the high limestone places
the lonely places gold
and black with the sun moving
through them moving with us
toward this moment of intent?

Harvest

Already the day
is on the turn as all these days
are on the turn
the light that rose up like
the odour of plums and of vines

beginning its descent
into the earth returning
laden with the voices
of roofers the calls
of blackbirds barks of dogs

hunting beyond the river
who pass between trees
passing to and fro
their shadows are unclear
they do not see themselves

it is we who see them
remembering the dark
as the light turns to the source
again turning once more
to the orange earth.

The Kingdom

Within this absolute
morning stillness
the creatures on their errands
are making sure
their estate is unchanged
by the gone night
is correct and whole the jays
calling dogs sorting
the fine morning smells
meanwhile beyond and in
all of this the stillness
which means a start which means
that everything is changed
and yet it stays the same
the creatures understand this
at the same time they
are uncertain their witness
is astonishment
who crowd the peaceable
mountain who inhabit
these limestone fields
as if in a dream
of plenty as if the beasts
hungered and fed as easily
as the soul
among its imagined
fields woods and farms.

Song Of Those Who Are To Come

We who are to come
to whom you owe this field
these trees this changing sky
to whom you owe these walls

that have comforted you
that will comfort us
because you made them
to be a shelter for us

although we need no shelter
having the field the trees
the changing sky to move
around us in their great

circuit we who come
out of that time when all
changing things will have their rest
we bless you

our parents wandering
the valley as if you
have just arrived as if
you understand nothing.

Arcades

In the morning air
voices fill and empty
beside the barn under
the walnut trees
one continual linked pouring
the way arcades go
linking and pouring linked
and poured their speech is one
continual discourse
raising hands to gesture
speaking on and on
in the shade under
the cypress trees they do not
know the morning or the evening
when it comes
they only know this speaking
that rises and falls
in them like song.

Collateral

Slow on cooling
July air
comes the siren's
homeless cry
as if the land
itself were lifted

as if farms
and tracks heaved
themselves up
(streaming
with branches
and wild flowers)

as if we were
held up to sky
all this lowland
airbase country
copses and fields
gardens and lanes

and what should we
expect or want
being complicit
say the spills
of sunlight say
the threshing leaves.

Zoi

*Evening star, bringing back everything the bright
dawn scattered* – SAPPHO

Perfectly at home
street dog the colour
of coffee you forget
yourself leaning on me

young dog the colour
of Greek coffee you lean
on me like a child
wanting to be picked up

wanting a home in my
lap wanting my coffee
(maybe you want me)
perfect in every part

pricked and appointed ears
and nose and tail you danced
your courtship dance on the bare
earth and now tired child

you come for rest and comfort
asking without shame
because there is no shame
as once Sappho taught you.

Bear Dancing

What is bear and what
is the dancing man
inside the bear skin what sweat
and what stink of tallow

hang between the man
and the old skin he wears
inside which the man dies
as bear is reborn

why does man put on
bear why raise him
again from darkness raise doubt
out of the dark

and who dances whom
when like a hand
dipped in a wound the fear
is danced over and over?

Caries

Little hole little well
of dark staining the lacquer
of my tooth little confessor
coming close and coming close

why are you pursuing me
interrogator of the nerve
in its garden of blood
and moisture its long sleep

what secrets can my nerve
confess to you what do you want
of us your drill
and file still thrillingly in play

and how shall I appease you
a god's dark eye
going to and fro and going
even in the secret places?

Before Dawn

All the world is hidden
          and human dreams and dog
dreams stream up
          together from the warm

bed like a praise song
          but what could be sung
in this stunned silence
          though the fields are sown

with small tracks where creatures
          stir and sniff
chafing thin blood
          through the webs of veins

and though birds watch
          from secret places
we guess and almost hear
          these are only rumours

nothing we worry about
          now will worry us
when we're old these griefs
          will be rumours too

and when William says you're like
          my daughter would be if
I had one some old wound
          is weeping sweetness

let his childlessness be healed
        with a praise song let him
know the hidden creatures
        of our dreams and of the fields

as he has known
        them all already
he has seen the shivering
        small hearts the eyes

that watch him as he watches them
        year after year
he praises them with his eyes pale
        like a December sky.

Christmas Tree

Larch carries the dark between its branches
in memory of the first darkness

this is sacrifice   a spiny embrace
that raises welts around your neck

Birthstone

Opals my grandmother loved, opals
    kept in musty boxes, velvet and dust
        and touch-me-not mystery –

the stuffy interior out of Doctor Freud
    and Grandma among her trophies
        sliding on the opal ring, sliding

the opal necklace between her fingers – something
    sensual, dirty almost, in her pleasure
        and the opals with their each way facets

their hard-to-believe fairground glitter were dirty
    too: foreign, vulgar even, I thought
        with a tremor I didn't realise

was sexual, was shame because I saw
    how the colours shone inside each like old coins
        in a vitrine, and how like old coins the stones

were stained by something, rumour or violence, she found thrilling;
    opals that are my birthstone, that I
        inherit with the rest of it –

tea service, couch, blue plush boxes
    the crooked glancing character of defect
        everything displayed like clues that afternoon

in the dark, overheated flat
    South Coast England nineteen eighty-something
        gone like a summer storm above the sea.

Syringe

Such sweetness. And such loneliness.
The needle's fine
Nurse Love slips it in –
her lightness of touch, her quickness –

brings me my joy.
Pain comes singing
down the vein

its high erratic song
pealing in the darkness of my room.

Insulin

for Fran

A face like her own
in the darkened window. Night
where the eyes should be

*

She touches the glass.
It too is damp
and cold

*

She smells of salt.
Her breast in the stranger's hand
is the colour of salt cod

*

A pulse throbs at her neck. Her colour
rises and rises
the blood unstoppable

*

Blood underlines the cut
approvingly. Out of fleshy pallor –
this scribbled response

*

She smells of salt. As if
the smell of her conception
were still on her

*

In the darkness in bed at night
hilarity switches tracks
and comes swerving back – lights blazing

*

White socks and Chinese skipping.
Under the school uniform she hides
a tiny grown woman: a poppet

*

Sparkle Frances, sparkle!
Her sparkle comes out staring
and wide-eyed

*

She smells of salt. As if preserving
cold salt spray
the cold of her birthplace

*

Little vixen
with her hot breath
and cunning

*

No-one can hear the *thrum-thrum*
of her heart.
No-one hears it pause

*

The human body is a heavy machine.
Such stillness
when the motor shudders and stops.

Leap

Like autumn when it
changes when
the breeze begins
its new idea

and cool air slips
between the roses
(yes this is
the turn) and when

the colours
in the garden
all withdrawn
and muted seem

to be a copy
of themselves
the hollyhocks
freckled with bites

meaning that summer's
over meaning
that things change
but you love change

how good it is
the end of rapture
cool and long
like the first evening drink.

Air Show

We live harmoniously
between the carrots
in their beds
and the lettuces

between the dogs sleeping
in their kennels
and the clouds whose gathering
thunder

is only fighter jets
in mid-display –
the dogs stir and twitch
but sleep is sweet

it comes pouring in
filling the ears
and filling up the lungs
like a great wind

bringing news of summer
with it bringing
a blue perfume
a great opening.

Morning

All morning it remains
morning by the cistern
and down the field to the river
where the green woodpecker

crosses and re-crosses her grass
all morning the morning
rests among ferns and ivy
in the cistern corner

or shows itself as brightness that casts
no shadow as when
Giotto painted world over
and over being young

in that young moment of our minds –
centuries old by now –
when morning was God everywhere
and all at once.

Fresco

Those long-dead painters
must have thought
it was impossible
to remake the world
however tender the flowers
and birds they left

lightly suspended
in tempera
whose modest visible
brushstrokes are like
a hand put out to touch
the other world

they inhabit now
or this painted world
that they re-enter
coming with us
who stand waiting for us
in the doorway.

Migraine

A great unease...
as if you caused the storm
as if your body
were you its strange
clay its dirt-pressure filling
up the head

where the brain's tender tatters
cleave to themselves
poor brain and eyes poor cranium

Somewhere in a forest tender
shadows pass
between the leaves that turn
as they turn marvellous
and indescribable
all these birds and small creatures

Bora

The light on the windowsill
is only half the light you dreamt of
but the wind soughing below you
is the sea that soughed all round you
in your first sleep

all day the wind soughs below you
in the trees and in your mind's ear
sound of distance and of home
making its promise that the breath
you hear is your own

Your own breath and far away
a remembered hillside of trees
where a breeze moved night and day
not touching you not stirring you
speaking its dream song

speaking its dream language even
then you knew it wasn't native
landlocked there among the trees
that it disturbed that it haunted
with long-gone breath

Stone Fruit

My trees are troubled by a wind
that blows from the heart
of each, a troubled wind
speaking the word *loss*

taking a breath to speak the word
again – *loss* –
as if it were the only word
and oh the swaying heartwood

Parsifal

The stag painted on the bowl
has leafy branching antlers
the huntsman could hide in them
et in arcadia ego

but this stag knows he carries death
in his green antlers
he raises the tree of life
raises the cup of death

between the trees in mid-winter
as arrows stream like rays
among the dead trees
from the cupped and risen sun

my spoon chimes on the stag's chest
on the golden heart
he carries between lines of black glaze –
his upraised golden heart!

Abscess

This is the raging stranger
in your mouth this
is the tongue as flaming sword
it isn't prophecy

when fire fuses the bones
that build your face you know
the wild bacteria
are here to force a home

in your cheek and jaw
you know they speak
instead of you they forge you
once again the pain

returning to the places
it knows best the little
places the hot places
like a truth.

Dusha

Black lurcher she comes trotting
eagerly and now she strolls
ahead her neck proud
waving her tail's black banner

hound descended from hounds
her black ensign sewn
with white her eager footing
bred to prance

between the legs of blazoned horses
she remembers and we forget
the smell of blood
always in her muzzle.

Albania

What do they talk about
kicking off their flip-flops
spreading out carrier bags
father and son who pass
a round loaf to and fro
and face the coast our ferry
works along for hours
steady as going on foot
yes they seem to say
we know about going
on foot we have learnt
steadiness in lives
not much visited
by wonder working lives
which sacrifice us yet
do not extinguish us
here we are carried
over the shining sea
and just like in stories
our beautiful women
are waiting just one day
away just one more day.

Night Train

Voices rise and fall
in a carriage floating
brightly through the dark.

Voices clustered voices
overlaid in patterns
like birdsong or weather

don't make them mean something
let them rise and fall
as if unconsoled.

Unconsoled

Over again this crooning
of doves in trees
they croon like the kindly
brow of day bent

over us protecting us
doves I heard
from my bedroom window
in that bright morning

before the others woke
brightness in the trees
doves with their
song of contentment

who are they telling
and who is in their care
when they stroke the forehead
of the little wood?

A PATH BETWEEN THE TREES

A Path Between The Trees

Who made this path
that passes under
ash and elder
bare brown flank
between the nettles
earth's warm skin
worn smooth by something
moving here
repeatedly
rust smell beneath
the leafy smell
odours of tea
and the rank stink
of rotting stems
nothing is frank
in the half shade
under the trees
where the path
moves past itself
over and over
the same gesture
you can almost
see it flicker
through the green
shadows where trees
line a path.

Cob

The way we used to live
in the old house a house
whose thick walls curved like the living
flanks of beasts

do you remember curving walls
the deep-set windows like
a kind of hope their light
white as the whitewashed walls

that someone made from living
things from straw and hair
and took the teeming mud
salted with living things

in tiny constellations
which hung round us there
baked with the dreaming hair
of horses the corn stalks

that crackled underfoot
and in the hand as they
were cut the mysteries
of domesticity

are also sacrifice
each kitchen knife shining
like joy they took the mud
and baked it as you might

a loaf made from corn
because the crust of things
rises and falls like breath
in the flanks of beasts.

Stone House

Really what I want
is to return
again and again
to a source
that's inexhaustible
and daily

but not a spring not ever
water which is
labile and cold which I
don't trust seeing
the glitter fall apart
in my hand

feeling my hand grow cold
I mean a wall
warm with the sun thick with it
like shelter
a wall thickly curved
and made by hands

whose gestures I could make
in my turn
in turning to a wall
its orange flank
glowing in the late light
behind nettles

and under elder trees
the source is love
I think but huge and abstract
this too a house
whose roofless rooms become
part of the wood

whose fire is choked with brambles
and wild apple
and with anemones
those lucky stars
pouring through doors and windows
and through the wall.

River

This room for example
this ordinary room
that flows away from you
never at rest
it flows and flows as if
everything dissolved
in the muddy blues
and greys of watercolour –
even this bright morning
already stained already
running away.

Blue

It isn't difficult
but it isn't here
blue lining the shadows
of the trees on summer grass

blue trees on hills
which mean something that goes
on and on the future
is it or the past

in the sunlight
of a day that isn't here
it's over there a day
leading the eye as if

the sun were just a spotlight
and under that blue pelt
the woods fomented dreams
going on endlessly.

Noli Me Tangere

You want to touch
of course you do
who wouldn't want
to touch the close-locked
scales on the snake's
anguine back

who wouldn't want
to grab the bear's fur
sinking hands
into coarse soft
roots that reek
of lanolin

who doesn't want
to stroke the actual
stone the weathered
bluestone marked
by chisels as if
only this year

wanting to touch
something that's shifting
out of sight
even as you
recognise it
if you do

you couldn't say
is it brightness
or a shadow
passing through
the pattern where things
stand and wait

for what is moving
there already
passing so close
it could almost
touch them
as it goes.

Field

after Samuel Palmer

White and green the hayfield
rises past my knees

like a summer storm
rising in the trees
it threshes a sweet smell
out of itself it soughs
away uphill.

And through its stems the creatures
track their errands

dark as the veins that track my calves
the hayfield sighs and stirs
and closes over itself
taking its miraculous light
into itself.

Mist

And you too when you're
alone or think
you are your stranger's eyes
cloud over

the way cloud blooms
on the hill opposite
our open window
bringing the new smell of rain

bringing the remembered
smell like something
luminous
light lying in the cloud

as if we both remembered
once in a deep lane
the smell of wet brambles
the new smell of earth

and how far away
home seemed then the lane
led to it cloudily
I thought but in the deep

green lane there was
only earth's wet heart
lightly scaled with scree
ragwort and nettles dark

with water dark and glowing
in the lane to school
and you were not yet born
and only I remember.

At The River

And are you still my guide
where the brown
river moves
slowly under trees

where the field curves down
to brown water
and pike move
slowly under the shadows –

is someone watching there
is someone there
watching the water
move and stay move and stay?

Avenue

You wake and find yourself
dreaming you walk
an avenue of trees
whose canopies

stir with the vagueness of dream
it seems
as though the time to come
must be a wind

stirring the leaves coming
from far away
in the west where a coast
shimmers vaguely

with surf shimmering like leaves
their white froth
spends itself
unimportantly

all this is very far
away
and you are very small
the air is deep

and you are far down in its valley
walking
the pale dust path walking
against the wind.

Here

Now this is achieved
what do you think of
under the red roofs
of the valley

under a blue sky
that carries with it
the promise that nothing
will change that here

time comes to a stop
leaving you
to hear the evening breeze
and the cicadas

in their eternal present
no dream
but limitless clarity
the promise

that you will go on here
even after
you have left although
you just arrived.

The Catch

You want – but something
holds you back
(voices in the
undergrowth

the cold shift
of a shadow)
something walks
beside you something

that was always
there a shadow is it
like your skin
and you remember

when you were
a child how each night
shadows met
across the grass

each night they met
to swallow time
the light put out
in each grass stalk

the story broken
that you'd told
yourself as you lay
in the brief

brightness
between the trees.

Acknowledgements

Some of these poems first appeared in *The Spectator, New Statesman, Poetry London, Temenos, World English Poetry,* Bengal Editions (Dhaka), *Interlitq* (Buenos Aires), *La traductière* (Paris), *Literara Romania* (Bucharest), *Viata Romanescu* (Bucharest), *Vsesvit* (Kiev), *Literaturnyy Ohlyad* (Kiev), *Kyiv* (Kiev), *Curator Aquarium* (Stockholm), *Istok* (Niš), *Ars Interpres* (Stockholm), *The Alhambra Calendar* (Brussels), *Poems for Camden Homeless Shelter* and *A festschrift for Katherine Gallagher.*

'Bear Dancing' was commissioned by BBC Radio 4 for *Postcards from the Village.* 'Night Train' and 'Neighbours' were commissioned by Magdalene College Cambridge Festival of Sound. 'Birthstone' was commissioned by *Intelligent Life.* 'Drowned Man' was commissioned by the Royal Society of Literature for *On Shakespeare's Sonnets Now* (The Arden Shakespeare/ Bloomsbury, 2015). 'Bora', 'Dusha', 'Zoi', 'Street Music' and 'Unconsoled' were commissioned by Wandsworth Archives and published in *Address Book* by Rack Press in association with Roehampton Poetry Centre. 'Stone Fruit' is from *Tree Carols,* set by Sally Beamish, commissioned by the Coull Quartet/ Roderick Williams/Warwick Arts Centre. 'Clothesline' is from *Paradise Row,* commissioned by Poet in the City/Archives for London for *Through the Door.* Earlier versions of some of these poems appeared in *Poetry Ireland.* Some of these poems were included in *Volta,* trans. Ioana Ieronim (Tracus Arte, Bucharest, 2015), *Preskochtii,* trans. Minja Golubovic (Kycha Poesia, Banja Luka, 2015) and *Marevo,* trans. Yuri Burjak (Kiev, 2015).

I am very grateful to the I.A. Literary Association, Slovenia, for a Writer's Fellowship at Škocjan, which enabled completion of this manuscript.